AF624801

Heartbreak, Hymns & Hope

Poems from a Bronx Heart, Still Beating Through The Wreckage.

Eric Michael Grant

BookLeaf Publishing

India | USA | UK

Made with ❤ on the BookLeaf Publishing Platform
www.bookleafpub.in
www.bookleafpub.com

Dedication

To my mother, Nancy.
You carried the weight of the world on your back and still managed to raise us with fierce love and unbreakable spirit, even while wrestling with your own demons. Your strength, though imperfect, was everything. I see you now with gentler eyes, and I thank you for your fight, your fire, and your heart. Rest in eternal peace Ma.

To my children Perrice, Dominique, Lauryn and Eric Jr.
You all inspired me to be a better person at different times of my life. I am filled with gratitude in watching you grow from babies to adults.

My Grandma Ruth, my Aunts, my Cousins, my Daughters and the partners who walked beside me through seasons of joy and heartbreak. You raised me in your own ways, piece by piece. You softened me when the world tried to harden me.

You taught me tenderness, resilience, and how to love even when it hurt.

This book, this journey, this heart is shaped by each of you. You are all my 'Bronx Queens'.

Thank you for helping me become the man I continue to grow into.

With love and reverence,

--Eric

Preface

"Heartbreak, Hymns & Hope" is a poetic mixtape of survival—written from fire escapes, Bronx stoops, and quiet moments in various States, scribed between the chaos and confusion. These are poems born of the Bronx: where heartbreak isn't just a feeling, it's a foundation. But from the rubble rises rhythm. These verses carry the weight of loss, the power of resilience, and the sacred music found in even the hardest places.

This collection explores a life filled with regret, shame, longing, and the stubborn hope for joy that refuses to die. These poems are not just words on paper; they're fragments of a man who has loved deeply, lost heavily, and endured.

Love, for me, has always been a complicated road. I've held it close and watched it slip away. I've mistaken it for safety, chased it in silence, and sometimes, walked away from it without fully understanding why. But through it all, I've remained open to its return.

Loss came early in my life—loss of stability, loss of innocence, loss of people I loved. Some left by choice. Others were taken too soon. And yet, in the wreckage, I found something quietly sacred: survival. A kind of emotional muscle memory that kept me moving forward, even when standing still seemed easier. Perseverance is the thread running through every page here. The Bronx raised me with sharp edges. Life softened some of them, love dulled others, but the fight—that inner fire—remained. These poems are the result of that persistence, the willingness to keep searching, to keep writing, to keep feeling.

If you've ever felt like you gave your all and still came up empty...
If you've ever been loved, left, or lost in between...
If you're still standing, still open, still searching—
Then maybe these words will feel like home.
--Eric

Acknowledgements

No book is written alone, and this one is no exception. To my late mother, Nancy—thank you for your sacrifices, your strength, and your love, even when the world was pulling you under. You gave more than you had, and somehow, you gave us enough.

To the strong women who shaped me—my grandmother, my aunts, my cousins, and the partners who walked beside me through different seasons—you've each poured something into my soul. You've taught me resilience, compassion, and how to keep my heart open in a world that often demands the opposite. This work carries your fingerprints.

To my siblings—you know the roots we share, the weight we've carried. Your presence has always reminded me where I come from, and who I write for.

To my children: Perrice Armon, Dominique Chanel, Lauryn Savoy, and Eric Michael, This book is a testament to my deep love for all of you. Not a day goes by where I don't think about each of you, even if my presence was lacking in the physical. You are my legacy and greatness is in each of you and I am so proud.

To my Ex-Wife Christina who offered up tough love over our 21 year marriage. Through the ups and downs you were always my biggest cheerleader, you saw the talent in me and challenged me to show my worth. I was a man lost and couldn't find a way back to myself and ultimately, us.

To my new friends who assisted me on my healing journey by inspiring me to be free. Free from judgement, free from negativity and complacency. I am forever inspired.

To every friend who listened, who encouraged me to keep writing, and who saw value in my voice—thank you for believing in these words before they had a home.

And to the readers—whether you came for love, loss, or something in between—I hope you find a piece of yourself here, and leave with a little more light.
With gratitude,

--Eric Michael Grant

1. . From A Time

I come from a time
when the world spun slower,
33 1/3 or 45 to be exact
Where keeping it Reel to Reel
Was poppin' in an 8 track

Back when truth wore fat laces
and breakbeats cracked concrete.
We weren't just kids—we were pioneers
with boomboxes for hearts
and cardboard or linoleum
for dance floors.

I grew up where the houses leaned in close
like they were listening
to the rhythm of our lives.
Where brick dust and broken glass
Became our sidewalks.
We were piled in high
And stacked up tight

Living in long lines for those
lactose treasures

We spit verses
in cipher sessions,
palms slapping on hoods like hand drums,
banging out rhythms on the metal
as if we could summon our future
with rhyme and percussion.

BOOM BOOM BAP
BAP BOOM BOOM BAP –
echoed in my head for hours
It's the cipher,
still circling.
Still sacred.
Still ours

When the sun dipped low,
we really came alive–
headed to the park after dark,
where the DJ turned dusk
into electricity that was stolen.
And every bass drop
was a heartbeat shared
between friends and enemies alike.

Our stories of pain resonated through play
through stairwells and alleys,
Through courtyards and backyards—
etched in every echo
of a shelltoe stomp,
every bruise, scrape, cut, broken bone
meant something. We were OUTSIDE!

I remember the air
smelling like spray paint,
skunk, and broken dreams.
When the sound of graffiti
was a gospel hymn
and every tag on a train
was a prayer whispered to the city.
Walking the tracks after dark
Heading to the lay ups
where the trains slept for the night
Awoken by my fat tipped magnum 44
TAGGED for the world to see.

And that first puff of weed
A euphoria of smiles and giggles
Feelings of happiness
Feelings of freedom.

We wore our Kangols like crowns,

Hop-Hop in our veins,
and gold chains that didn't just shine—
they told history,
Ancestry melted down
and molded into something
too loud to ignore.

You know you SEE US!

We didn't walk,
we fucking Bopped
like each block was a runway,
like each streetlight
was a spotlight
on our dopeness.

You know you fucking SEE US!

Because when the world said,
You can't
we said,
Watch this!
Then spun on our backs
and rewrote gravity
And defied logic.
Our DNA the blueprint of
Well, EVERYTHING!

We didn't have algorithms.
We had rhythm.
We had soul.
We had the courage
to make noise
when silence felt safer.

So no—this ain't nostalgia.
It's legacy.
It's that New York voice
Accent Thick
Swag Girthy.
Still rising
from brick dust and broken glass,
to cracked floors and urine stained halls
Yeah, that's Where I'm from—
But this is where I'm at.
Happy
Healthy
Humble - and
Honored to be from The Bronx!

2.. Light Sheep

I was born
into a tribe of melanin magic—
deep roots, strong noses, rich skin like mahogany and
midnight oil.

But me?

I was the light sheep.
Head full of curly hair
like confused question marks,
a long nose that never quite fit the family portrait.

My reflection?
A remix.
A mystery.
They'd call me light-skin or redbone
like it was a punchline,
a side note in a song I didn't know the words to.

Yeah I'd smile,

laugh even—
but inside, I was searching for pieces of a man
I never met.
My biological father—a ghost in my DNA,
a blank space on the family tree
that no one could fill,
and no one dared to explain.

I watched my cousins walk in their dark skin
like it was armor.
I walked in mine like it was a question—
like I had to prove I belonged.
I loved my people,
but I didn't know if I was of my people.

And every time I looked in the mirror,
I asked:
Who am I really?
What did he look like?
Did he leave me this nose, this hair, this hole in my identity?

I am the light sheep,
But let this be heard—
my blood runs just as deep,
my soul still hums the rhythm
of a people who made beauty from struggle,

and power from pain.

But still—
I search.
Not for him,
but for me.
Who am I really?

3.. Cracked Hearts

As if overnight, I watched her fade,
A Queen once bright, now dim, betrayed.
Glass in hand, dreams turned to smoke,
The lullaby of hope she slowly broke.

Bronx stoops cried as mothers wept,
While silent pain in children crept.
Whole homes shattered, love turned cold,
Warm hearts stolen, so many souls sold.

It wasn't just my mother's fall
A nation cracked, a siren's call.
Blocks were once filled with joy
Now just pipes and vials – the new toy

Still, I hold her in my heart,
A broken past I can't depart.
But from the rubble, I did rise—
From visions of loss, to hopeful eyes.

4.. She Blooms

She was wildfire scorched, untamed,
ashes in her lungs, but she still remained.
Roots ripped up, storms tore through,
but her rain of tears taught her to renew.

She is the mountain, unshaken, tall,
cracked by quakes but will never fall.
Winds have howled, tried to break her soul,
but she stands like stone—powerful, whole.

She is the river, winding, wild,
cutting through rock with a knowing smile.
She bends, she twists, she carves her way,
turns broken ground into sacred clay.

She is the seed, buried but strong,
the dark tried to hold her, but she proved it wrong.
Through dirt, through weight, through endless night,
she reached for the sun—she rose in the light.

She Blooms

5.. Playing House

We were just kids
Who thought we were grown
running wild in shell toes and hand-me-down wisdom.
We played Run, Catch & Kiss
Even before we knew how to.

That first kiss?
Well... it was clumsy magic.
Fire and nerves in the same breath.
Her lip trembled like mine,
but we held it together like
we'd practiced in dreams
or in mirrors
when no one was looking.

We played house. I'll be Husband
You my spouse.
Then came that first touch—
fingers curious, unsure,
like turning pages in a forbidden book.

Heartbeats pounding while body parts
Grew thicker than the bass in the car
we weren't supposed to be in.

We thought we knew.
We thought love lived in sweaty palms
and the silence after a deep breath,
right before you say "I like you"
like it's a dare.

We'd talk on the phone for hours
Refusing to be first to hang up,
You hang up, no you first
Satisfying, like a quenched thirst.

We were just kids—
pretending we were grown,
growing up too fast,
chasing feelings
with no map,
no manual,
just hormones and hip-hop lyrics.

We thought we knew what love was...
but it was just the beginning.
And maybe,
just maybe—

that’s what made it beautiful.

6.. Glass Piped Dreams

In dim-lit dens of dope and despair,
whispers of hope vanished like smoke through stale air,
Families fractured like broken mirrors on the floor,
Each shard a story—bad luck, bloodied, bitter, and sore.

Crack came cruel, like a serpent slithering in the seams,
Stealing sleep, tempting souls and slicing through dreams.
Fathers and Mothers turned fiends, the children bore the brunt
Trading love for lighters, the high becoming the only want.

Silver spoons vanished, not from mouths but drawers,
Pawned for little rocks behind pawnshop doors.
TVs and stereos torn from their homes,
For a hit that hums through marrow and bones.

Little hands hugged hollow hopes,
While parents prowled like wolves on dope.

Violence was vintage, passed down like clothes,
In houses where love no longer grows.

Knuckles cracked like the rocks in the pipe,
Brothers beat brothers under flickering lights.
Granny and Auntie wept as uncles stole rings,
Even the baby's rattle could get something .

The pipe preached louder than a Pastors prayer,
A gospel of glass, a breath of despair.
Smoke spiraled like a noose from the lip
Each drag a dagger, each puff a whip.

Hope got holed up in high-rise hells,
Where lullabies were sirens and shotgun shells.
The devil danced in a dealer's disguise,
Selling sweet salvation that'll roll back your eyes.

This was the era of theft and tears,
Of cracked-out chaos and butchered years.
Where love was a luxury too pricey to hold,
And hearts were bartered for bits of gold.

A war not of weapons, but want and withdrawal,
Where families were fractured, futures would fall.
The crack era carved severe scars in the soul
Shit— back then-- even the scars would be sold!

7.. Grandma's Hands

Grandma was jazz—
improvised grace,
Shuffling with rhythm in orthopedic shoes
that danced down linoleum aisles
of the A&P and corner bodegas.
She was a Diva like Ella herself
with a hand full of coupons
and a head full of dreams.

She'd pull me along like a co-conspirator,
my small hand swallowed by her leather-worn grip
as we hit the local number spot.
She'd call out random numbers –
scribbling hope on slips of carbon paper
like prophecy.
Coded whispers only the streets understood.
I watched her wheel and deal
in quiet alleys of survival
while my mother was, well most days I never knew,
Grandma was teaching life lessons

The art of the hustle
The art of kindness
The art of being unapologetically you.

.....And her purse, it was a magic portal—
Mary Poppins by way of The Bronx.
Stuffed with receipts, crumpled bills,
old church programs,
a coin purse and cigarettes.
But way down deep—-
The promise of something sweet.
"Don't tell your mother," —she'd whisper
behind a cumulus cloud of smoke
that hung in the air forever,
her Pall Mall dangling
like punctuation at the edge of her stories.
Unfiltered truths poured from her lips
while ash clung stubbornly to the edge of time.

The candy—
butterscotch, golden and crinkled
like little suns trying to be holy—
tasted like church pews and bus rides,
like something too old to be good,
but too good to throw away.
So I'd savor it slowly,
face contorting from writhing in revulsion

to a puckered grimace.
The sacrament secretly between us
made it worth it.

Grandma's hands—
time machines,
making magic behind the Singer,
crafting garments of splendor,
seamlessly sewing styles of today
with the couture'd style of a past time.

Her voice was gravel and gospel,
and when she coughed,
it shook the windows
like thunder too proud to apologize.
But oh, when she laughed,
it cracked the sky—
a song with no sheet music,
just instinct and soul.

She gave me rebellion dressed as love,
gave me history wrapped in cellophane,
gave me herself—
flawed, fierce, free.
And in those hands,
smelling of tobacco and Ben-Gay,
I was always safe,

always seen,
always sacred.

8.. Right On Time

People come in like waves–
crashing, calm, or just brushing the sand
no one by mistake, even if we don't understand.

Some arrive like sunrises–warm,
spilling light in the cracks where we thought we'd die.
Blessings wrapped in skin and smiles,
teaching us how to live again, how to try.

Others?
They're storms.
Toxic tongues, hard truths,
mirrors that cut more than reflect
but damn, didn't we need the wound
to know we were bleeding?

Some just... exist.
Background jazz in the waiting room of your life,
filling the silence 'til the real song plays.
But even they–

they were time's stories,
holding space 'til the next page turned.

We say "bad timing,"
but what is time except the lie we use
to explain away things we don't understand?
Time is life, and life is a classroom
with no syllabus.

So bless the blessings.
Curse the curses.
Sit with the space-fillers.
They all came on purpose.
Right on time.
Whatever that means.

9.. Grace Yourself

I was raised where the concrete cracked like broken promises,
In the Bronx, where dreams are made of duct tape and defiance.
Where the sirens sang lullabies and the corner knew my name
Before my mother ever whispered "It's gonna be okay."

But it wasn't.

Not when I stood soaked in shame,
Pants piss-wet from fear,
The Boy Scout leader's hose cold and merciless,
While the troop laughed like wolves.
A young boy baptized in humiliation,
Before I ever learned what pride was.

Mom dukes was a goddess in my childish eyes,
Then I watched her trade hope for a crack pipe,
Selling light just to taste the dark.

And I—her son—became the easy target
For a man who wore "father" like a costume.
He hit me with the weight of her sins,
His fists preaching sermons of misdirected rage.
I learned pain before puberty,
Learned silence before sleep.

Then came the girl.
I was fifteen; careless, scared, and stupid.
She carried life while I ran from it,
Like a boy could ever outrun a heartbeat.
I left her holding a future I helped make,
Never called, never looked back.
Now her silence echoes louder than my regret.

And the daughter...
Four years old when I disappeared,
Chose flight over fight,
Selfishness disguised as fear.
She's grown now.
And she wants nothing to do with the man who left.
I don't blame her.

My biggest regret.

You see, grace ain't free.
It's a war I fight every day

In the mirror.
Shame don't sleep,
And forgiveness don't answer unless you knock hard and often.

But I'm learning.
Slowly.
That even broken boys
Can still build bridges.
Even in the Bronx,
Where we learned to survive
Before we ever learned to live.

10.. Namesake

I gave you my name...
Written in black ink with trembling hands,
a prayer, a promise, a dare against time itself.

You, my son—
a living echo of every dream
I never spoke aloud.
And with that name,
I gave you everything I had...
and everything I fear.

There's a terror they don't tell you about
when they hand you your child—
it's not just the fear of falling,
it's the fear of you falling short.

The fear that somehow, some way,
this world, sharp and merciless,
might carve into you too deep—
and it'll be my fault.

Because isn't it always the father's fault?
If you hurt, it's because I didn't teach you how to fight.
If you break, it's because I didn't show you how to heal.
If you doubt, it's because I didn't make you believe hard enough.

Every scratch on your soul
feels like it bleeds from my hands.
They say the love for a child is unexplainable—
and they're right.
Because how do you explain
feeling your own heart
living in someone else's chest?

How do you explain the sleepless nights,
the quiet wars fought in the silence of your mind,
the prayers muttered like broken mantras
that you'll be enough,
that you'll teach him right,
that you'll keep him safe
without clipping his wings?

And God, the pressure—
to get it right every time.
Because this name you carry
isn't just letters stitched together—

it's my legacy,
my apology to the universe,
my desperate hope
that somehow you'll be more than me,
better than me.

But son—
if you ever fall,
know this:
it's not a mark of my failure,
and it's not the end of your story.
It's proof that you are living,
that you are fighting,
that you are trying to find your way.

And I will always be here,
arms scarred but open,
voice shaking but strong,
with a love so deep it defies words.

A love that hopes,
that fears,
that aches,
that believes.

A love that carries your name—

the name of mine—
into forever.

11.. Mind>Body

You ever had thoughts so deep
it sent shivers down your spine?
A sentence so smooth it traces
your curves like fingers over silk?

See, I don't just wanna touch you
I want to unravel you.
I wanna slide between the pages of your mind,
bookmark your insecurities
and highlight your dreams,
read you aloud till you moan metaphors,
and your sighs sound like similes.

See, I could trace the outline of your thighs,
but I'd rather trace the outline of your thoughts,
follow them like constellations,
connect the stars till I find
the universe inside you.

I wanna kiss you with questions,

leave bite marks of philosophy on your skin,
press my palms against the small of your intellect
until your body arches into understanding.

Let's turn wordplay into foreplay,
make love to the rhythm of our syllables,
let every consonant be our constant cadence,
and every vowel a possible sign,
like A E, I O U---
NO!, you owe me nothing.

And when you do tremble,
it won't just be from fingertips or tongues,
it'll be from ideas so raw
they set your skin on fire.
Because pleasure is fleeting,
but stimulation?
That lingers.

So, I don't just want your body,
I want your mind!

12.. Not Jaded, Never Faded

Not jaded, never faded,
or waiting on breath that's bated,
No longer tangled in the weight
of love that's overrated.
I walked through fire, felt the sting,
that hurt not overstated
Lessons learned, bridges burned,
yet here I stand—Elated.

No bitter words upon my tongue,
no grudges in my chest,
I lay resentment down to rest;
my heart deserves the best.
What's gone is gone, I won't look back
or curse the past in vain,
I rise above, embrace the light,
and dance beyond the pain.

Love is not a prison cell,
nor is it my demise,

It’s meant to lift, not chain the soul
or dim the hopeful skies.
So here I go, unburdened now,
no venom in my veins,
Not jaded, never faded—
just free from love in chains.

13.. Multilinguistic

I speak in tongues of touch,
words weaving
like weeping willows in the wind,
A cunning linguist
fluent in the dialect of desire,
and versed
in the art of anticipation.

Daring to make you feel
out of this World.
My hands trace constellations
across your skin,
mapping galaxies of longing,
Each fingertip a comet's kiss,
leaving traces of electricity
for eternity.

I articulate devotion
in the giving of gifts,
Like the earth offering spring

its first bloom,
Or the moon slipping silver
into the waves below.
Wrapped in ribboned intentions,
I leave tokens
like fallen leaves,
Sincere echoes of love
left to be found.

Acts of service flow from me
like rivers carving canyons,
A quiet reshaping
of the world for you.
I am the sun
breaking open the morning,
A light and warmth
that arrives before you even ask,
providing safety
from an often dark and cold world.

My words bloom
like multicolored tulips,
or like the faces
of innocent children
turned toward your light,
Poetry whispered in the wind,
planting roots in your soul.

I think your name
like lightning preceding a storm,
a symphony of sound
that follows the painting in the sky.
And time.
Time is the gravity that binds us,
Pulled together
like planets in a celestial tango.
Every shared moment
a meteor shower,
Each second
a shooting star burning just for us.
For as long as this World will have us.
I want you in my orbit.

I am fluent in the languages of love,
A polygamist of passion,
a whisperer of warmth,
A harbinger of human emotions
with true intention.
Who out there will I speak to?
And when I speak,
the universe will listen.
For I am the Love I deserve

14.. Unpacked Silence

I folded twenty three years into a cardboard box,
taped shut with the same hands
that once reached for hers in the dark.

Love doesn't always echo when it leaves—
sometimes, it vanishes
like a sound swallowed in snowfall.

We were a house with creaking floors
and photos on the walls that refused to forget.
Now, I walk barefoot through memories
like broken glass—carefully, deliberately—
bleeding only where I still feel.

Starting over feels like leaving home
for the first time, but older.
Not with a suitcase of dreams,
but with a ledger of lessons,
a roadmap etched in tears and tenderness.

I don't chase love now—I study it,
like a storm from a window,
learning its patterns, its silence,
its suddenness.
Yet still, unpredictable.

There is a son
nearly a man now, with eyes
that hold our best years.
He is the soft thread between what was
and what's next.
For him, I stayed steady
even when my hands shook
behind closed doors.

There is gratitude—sharp, honest—
like the final note of a song
that once played endlessly in our minds.
No regret, no bitterness,
Just reverence for the ache that taught me
who I am when I am alone.

Dating? Not yet.
Not until I can sit across from someone
without seeing ghosts in their smile.
Not until I can offer my heart
without wrapping it in apology.

This time, I want presence,
not just proximity.
Depth, not just declarations
Or surface level commonalities.

I want someone who doesn't fear the quiet,
who can dance in its rhythm with me,
who understands that love
isn't always light—it's also shadow.
And I want to meet myself there too—
fully, finally—
as the man I've been becoming
since the moment I said goodbye.

15.. A Rising Tide

She is not rain.
Rain comes and goes
And evaporates in the sun.
She is the Ocean
Deep trenched and volatile
With salt on her lips
and wreckage in her smile.
She is a current that never asks for
permission to flow.

She moves with the grace
of centuries.
Wet with memory,
slick with knowing,
still enough to cradle a man
in her calm,
Yet wild enough to swallow him whole without a trace.

He is not a stone.
Stones can be tossed aside

and skimmed across a lake.
He is a mountain.
Unyielding, deep veined and relentless,
a monument of strength and grandeur.
Edges sharp,
core hard like granite,
he's built himself
on never being moved.

Then, she...
she gathers at his foothills,
quiet at first.
A whisper along his cracks.
Just a splash at his base.

She does not knock.
She seeps in slowly.

With every pass,
she learns the ridges,
makes maps of his hardness
in the dark.
And then,
without warning,
she surges.

She wraps herself around him,

rises in waves,
the kind that don't just touch
but crash

And still he stands
until he can no longer.

When she crests
she shakes him.
Not with fury,
but with truth,
the truth that even stone
cannot hold
when the water surges through.

He shudders,
Quakes,
his stillness undone
by the force of her tidal wave-
not loud,
but deep.
A tsunami of passion.

And just like that,
the mountain breaks.
Not destroyed,
but revealed.

Reshaped by the flood
that he didn't anticipate.

And the Ocean
showed just how intense her waves
Could be, when there is
nothing left
to hold back.

16.. Sign O' my Times

I was born in '68,
right at the edge of soul and funk,
when the world was spinning on vinyl and revolution.
By 1980, I was 12 –
prepubescent, awkward,
still figuring out my Alphabet St.
...then I heard Baby...
track one, side two of For You,
and suddenly I knew more
than my body had lived.
That falsetto
That vulnerability
Prince wasn't just singing –
he was unlocking a room in me I didn't know existed.
A sensitivity and softness
Most men never dare to admit.
I Wanna Be Your Lover became my morning mantra.
Sexy Dancer played in my head
as I daydreamed through middle school math class.
While my peers chased Top 40,

Or Run-DMC,
I wandered down Paisley Park,
curious, a little strange, and proud of it –
because Prince made strange feel sacred.
He taught me
that you could wear whatever, hell,
Sometimes damn near nothing-
play guitar like Hendrix,
write songs like Lennon,
and still ride in on a Little Red Corvette.
He showed me that little light skinned boys
could be tender, loud, spiritual, carnal –
all in the same breath.
He made Controversy a lifestyle, not a scandal.
Dirty Mind cracked open when I was thirteen.
Hormones matched every synth riff.
It was rebellion, it was gospel, it was
permission to be a little wild – and want.
By '84, I was sixteen –
and Purple Rain baptized me.
Not just the music –
the movie, the mythology.
The Beautiful Ones had me
crying in the dark,
trying to reconcile my own
teenage heartbreak.
Computer Blue, Darling Nikki –

too grown for a teen,
but I was already in deep.
That purple, that passion –
etched in my spirit like vinyl grooves
And breakdance moves.
And then came Sign O' the Times.
Seventeen, going on soul survivor.
That record didn't leave my turntable for a year.
Title track hit home like a Cat 5.
If I Was Your Girlfriend –
I studied it like scripture.
The Ballad of Dorothy Parker
made me pay more attention
to the girls with quick wit,
not just the so called Cool girls.
And Adore?
That was how I wanted to
love someday –
sweat, tears, truth, all of it.
Slow,
Intentional,
Sexy as Fuck.
While others chased trends,
I followed a Raspberry Beret
through the backrooms of
musical possibility.
Rock. Funk. Jazz. Soul, Hip Hop, Psychedelia.

Because Prince wasn't one genre –
He was music itself.
Now I'm older,
but when I hear I Wanna Be Your Lover,
Or Sexy Dancer
I'm right back there –
a gapped toothed Bronx kid
with big ears and a bigger heart,
learning how to live out loud
because one man dared
to defy every box
and sing in falsetto truths.
Prince,
you were the soundtrack to my awakening,
my armor in adolescence,
my guide into authenticity.
You taught me how to groove,
how to cry,
how to cross boundaries with purpose.
You gave me Musicology before I had a word for it.
You showed me
how to be a Sign O' the Times
and not apologize for it.
Your lyrics weren't just music –
they were blueprints.
They gave me the courage
to put pen to paper,

to tell my own truths in rhythm and rhyme.

Because of you,

I don't just listen differently –

I write differently.

Fearless.

Free.

Fully myself.

Thank you.

RIP 0(+>

17.. Tune In

I'm out here,
Tuned in to a frequency
most can't find.
Not AM, not FM—
I'm talking heart-waves
and spirit static,
a love language that doesn't
need translation.

I've been searching
for connection
not just skin deep,
but soul to soul,
vibe-on-vibe,
eyes that say "I see you"
before lips even touch .

I want conversation
that dances—
not small talk,

but deep dives into dreams
and desires,
past lives and what if futures.
Words that feel
like goosebumps
on the inside of my mind.

I'm looking for you—
the one who feels
like déjà vu
Subconsciously envisioned
but brand new.
Someone who's
tired of pretending,
ready to get real, raw,
and beautifully unfiltered.

Give me your truths,
your kinks,
your chaos.
I'll give you mine.
Let's be wild and whispered,
tangled and untamed.
Match my freak—
not just in bed,
but in thought,
in spirit,

in how we yearn
for something more.

I know you're out there,
trying to tune in
tapping your foot to the same rhythm,
feeling this pull in your chest too.
If you hear this—
speak back.
I'm done broadcasting
into the void.
I want you on this wavelength.
No masks,
no apologies.

Just two energies colliding
exactly how they were meant to.
Unapologetically aligned.
Unforgettably wild.
Undeniably us.
If you're out there, Tune In!

18.. Rewired

I wake in a world that whispers worry before I even rise
—
But I decide,
To speak peace before panic,
Gratitude before grind,
To train my mind
like it's the gym,
'Cause strength starts from within.

See, thoughts are seeds—
And every I can't
is a weed
choking the bloom of I will.
But I've learned to be still...
To pause.
To breathe.
To feel.

Mindfulness isn't just quiet time—
It's reclaiming power in real time.

It's catching that storm before it spins,
And saying,
Not today,
I'm choosing calm again.

Positive thinking isn't fake smiles
or blind eyes,
It's recognizing the fear
then telling it: You don't live here .
It's daily reps of I am enough.
It's reprogramming that inner voice
to speak love when life gets tough.

So train the mind,
tend to the soul,
and watch how high you grow—
when you believe
you're already whole.

19.. High On You

I want to micro-dose
your kisses
and intravenously
get high on hugs.
No prescription needed–
your touch is the plug.

Call it love in milligrams,
truth in tiny hits,
you whisper in my ear
and my whole soul shifts.

I'm trippin' on your rhythm,
heartbeats sync in time,
each glance a hallucination,
each breath–sublime.

This ain't addiction,
it's a sacrament,
a sacred vibe

That's heaven sent.

So lean in—
be my therapy,
my chemistry,
my clear point of view
Cuz baby,
I'm just tryin' to stay high off the dose of you.

20.. Stained Glass & Uncushioned Pews

I grew up where the organ grinded
like a rolling tide of electrified sound,
deep and thunderous,
yet shimmering at the edges
like light through stained glass.

Harlem Sundays where hats were sharp as switchblades,
and pews packed people tighter than a pack of newports.
Where the A/C always seemed to be in the fritz,
and paper fans of MLK failed to make a cool breeze,
Where Sister Johnson caught the Holy Ghost at 11:15
sharp,
and Deacon Earl always caught some kind of fit by 11:30.

And the sermons—
A masterclass woven from breath and thunder.
The call and response,
The sporadic shouts
of praise and worship.

They said, Come as you are,
They said, God is love,
but kept a side-eye for boys who walked too softly
and girls who seemed too friendly.

The choir sang Jesus Loves Me,
but behind the scenes gossip
about Gary and Steve made its way around faster than
the collection plate,
and we passed that thang like a bad habit,
Granny giving her last few dollars with faith,
so the church could add to the never ending church fund,
while the roof in her apartment still leaked.

They said, "God don't like ugly,"
but somehow He was always around
when folks who acted the ugliest was saying
Come as you are.

I saw contradictions wrapped in choir robes,
watched holy hands slap sense into kids
on the A train on a Saturday,
then lift those hands to praise the Lord on Sunday.

It's a confusing cocktail—
Hallelujahs mixed with side-eyes,

love linked to conditions,
forgiveness preached but not practiced.

Yet Still, I clapped
Still, I danced.
I sang like salvation was on sale
and I needed a discount.

Because love was there too— So Much Love.

In the hugs,
In the after worship dinners,
In the tambourines
played by hands that held you
when the world wouldn't.

But maybe faith ain't a building,
or a man in robes,
or a verse yelled loud.

Maybe it's the quiet knowing
that Jesus does indeed love you too.
So I hold both:
The hymns and the hush-ups,
the hope and the hurt,
the Amen and the "Ain't this some mess?"

And still I pray—
Not to be perfect, but real.
Not to escape the questions,
but to ask them loud enough
that even Heaven can't ignore them.

21.. Bronx Queens

He came up in a world
of lace and lullabies,
Where wisdom wore aprons
and strength had soft eyes.

No boots stomped the floor,
no deep voice to obey,
Just lullaby lectures
and love on display.

Aunties, mothers, cousins—
his circle of grace,
Taught him the power of patience,
the warmth of a face.

He learned to listen
before he would speak,
To cherish the tender,
to cradle the weak.

He knew how to soothe,
how to sit with the storm,
How to weather the world
and still stay warm.

But in rooms where thunder
was praised as control,
He struggled to carve out
a powerful role.

No man to model
the steely-eyed stare,
Or teach how to lead
with a confident flair.

So when the world asked for brawn,
Or a vicious bite,
He offered an olive,
not ready to fight.

They called him too gentle,
too soft to be strong,
But kindness, he knew,
never steered him wrong.

Still, some nights he'd wonder,
in quiet and doubt,

What manhood would mean
if he'd mapped a new route.

Not alpha, not beta–
just fully, just real,
With softness that sharpens,
and strength he can feel.

A man made of women,
Inner strength, they've inspired,
Learning his way
without need for hellfire

To someone else's myth
of what makes a man rise.
He's whole in his heart,
with truth in his eyes.

A Man, raised by Bronx Queens

www.ingramcontent.com/pod-product-compliance
Lightning Source LLC
Chambersburg PA
CBHW051734130826
49812CB00033B/863
* 9 7 8 9 3 7 0 9 2 9 1 5 9 *